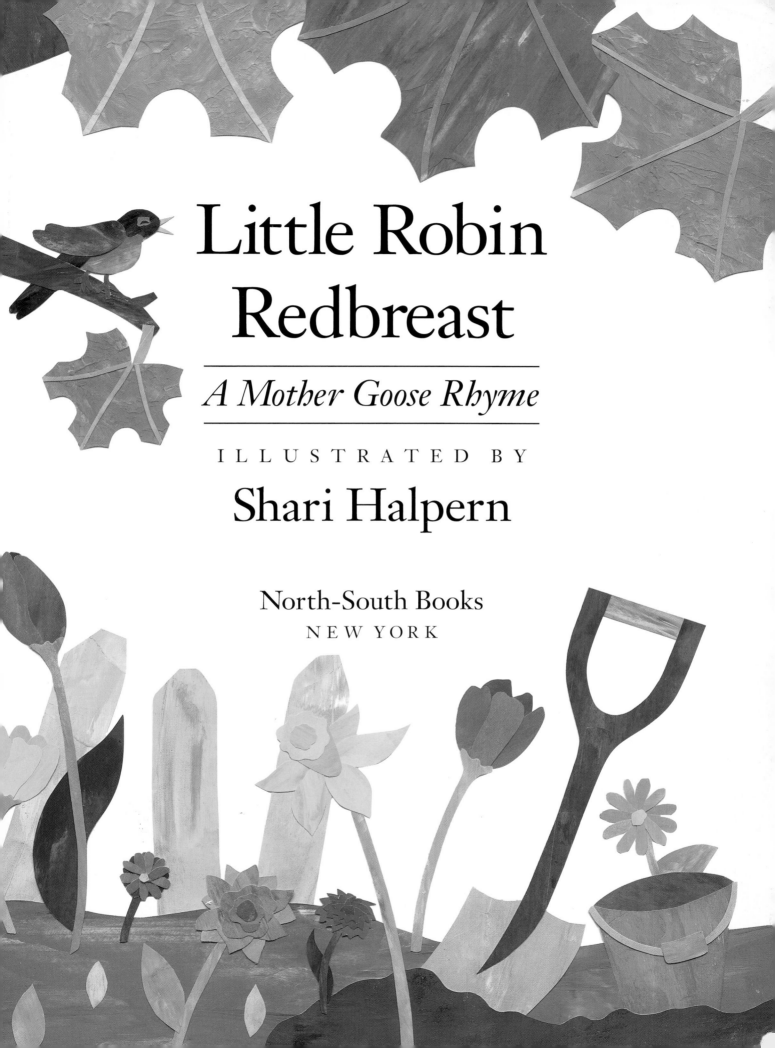

Little Robin Redbreast

A Mother Goose Rhyme

ILLUSTRATED BY

Shari Halpern

North-South Books
NEW YORK

Little Robin Redbreast
sat upon a tree,

Up went the Pussy-Cat,

and down went he,

Down came Pussy-Cat,

away Robin ran;

Says little Robin Redbreast:
"Catch me if you can!"

Little Robin Redbreast
sat upon a spade,

Pussy-Cat jumped after him,
and then he was afraid.

Little Robin chirped and sang,
and what did Pussy say?

Pussy-Cat said:

"Mew, mew, mew,"

and Robin flew away.

"Little Robin Redbreast" was one of the very first Mother Goose rhymes ever published. An early, bawdy version appeared about 1744 in the second volume of the earliest known collection of English nursery rhymes, *Tommy Thumb's Pretty Song Book*. Less rude versions followed in other children's books, but the verse as it is known today apparently first appeared about 1800 as a song written for pianoforte and published in London by the English composer Robert Birchall. He possibly took it from some now forgotten oral source. This was the first known version in which Robin Redbreast outfoxed the cat, and it soon passed into the lore of Mother Goose—with and without the music.

For Grandma Edna

Published in the United States by North-South Books Inc., New York.

Published simultaneously in Great Britain, Canada, Australia, and
New Zealand in 1994 by North-South Books, an imprint of
Nord-Süd Verlag AG, Gossau Zürich, Switzerland.
First paperback edition published in 1996 by North-South Books.

Library of Congress Cataloging-in-Publication Data
Little Robin Redbreast : a Mother Goose rhyme / illustrated by Shari Halpern
Summary: An illustrated version of the traditional rhyme
describing a robin's encounter with a cat.
1. Nursery rhymes. 2. Children's poetry. [1. Nursery rhymes.]
I. Halpern, Shari, ill. II. Mother Goose.
PZ8.3.L73467 1994
398.8—dc20 93-38760

A CIP catalogue record for this book is available
from The British Library.

ISBN 1-55858-247-9 (trade edition)
1 3 5 7 9 TB 10 8 6 4 2
ISBN 1-55858-248-7 (library edition)
1 3 5 7 9 LB 10 8 6 4 2
ISBN 1-55858-551-6 (paperback edition)
1 3 5 7 9 PB 10 8 6 4 2

The artwork consists of cut-paper collage, using paper
painted with acrylics. The type is Janson.
Typography by Marc Cheshire
Printed in Belgium